Nobody Taught Us This

Nobody Taught Us This

Matthew Petchinsky

1

Nobody Taught Us This: The Missing Human Manual for Money, Energy, and Self-Respect

By: Matthew Petchinsky

Disclaimer

Nobody Taught Us This:

The Missing Human Manual for Money, Energy, and Self-Respect is provided for **educational and informational purposes only**.

This book is **not** a substitute for professional advice of any kind, including—but not limited to—financial, legal, medical, psychological, therapeutic, or business advice. The concepts, frameworks, language, and examples presented throughout this work are intended to support **personal awareness, critical thinking, decision-making, and individual responsibility**, not to replace qualified professional guidance tailored to your specific circumstances.

Nothing in this book should be interpreted as a guarantee of financial outcomes, emotional results, energy improvements, or life changes. Any references to money, income, wealth, productivity, energy, boundaries, self-respect, or life systems are **conceptual models** designed to help readers examine patterns, assumptions, and behaviors—not prescriptions for action. Individual results will vary based on personal choices, external conditions, and implementation.

The author does not claim to diagnose, treat, cure, or prevent any medical, psychological, neurological, or emotional condition. If you are experiencing physical, mental, emotional, or financial distress, you are strongly encouraged to seek assistance from a qualified professional.

All decisions made based on the ideas in this book are made **solely at the reader's discretion and risk**. By reading this material, you acknowledge that you are fully responsible for your interpretations, actions, and outcomes. The author and publisher assume no liability for any loss, injury, hardship, or damages—financial, emotional, relational, or otherwise—that may result from the use or misuse of the information contained herein.

This book may challenge commonly accepted narratives around money, effort, productivity, obligation, and self-worth. Such challenges are offered in the spirit of **reflection and self-examination**, not instruction or coercion. Readers are encouraged to adapt, discard, or reinterpret any concept according to their own values, circumstances, and judgment.

By continuing to read, you affirm that you understand this work is a **conceptual manual, not a professional directive**, and that responsibility for application rests entirely with you.

Introduction

Why modern life feels harder than it should—and why that isn't your fault

If life feels heavier than it should, you are not imagining it.

You are not weak. You are not broken. You are not failing some invisible test that everyone else passed. What you are experiencing is the quiet consequence of a world that evolved faster than the human instruction manual ever did.

Modern life demands fluency in systems no one formally explains. Money systems. Energy systems. Social expectations. Attention economics. Emotional labor. Invisible rules about worth, productivity, and survival. Most people are dropped into these systems early, expected to "figure it out," and then quietly blamed when exhaustion, anxiety, or confusion sets in.

This book starts from a simple, stabilizing truth: **most people were never taught how to live sustainably—emotionally, financially, or mentally.** Not because of neglect. Not because of malice. But because there *was no manual*.

Previous generations passed down survival strategies that worked in slower, simpler environments. But the world shifted. Systems multiplied. Costs rose. Attention fractured. Responsibility increased while clarity disappeared. The gap between what is required to function and what is actually taught has grown wide—and most people fall into it without knowing why.

Nobody taught us how to manage money without shame.
Nobody taught us how to protect energy without guilt.
Nobody taught us how to build self-respect without dominance or submission.

Instead, we were given fragments. Advice without context. Rules without explanation. Pressure without instruction. When those fragments failed to hold, the failure was assigned to the individual.

This book rejects that narrative.

Nobody Taught Us This is not a motivation book. It does not ask you to hustle harder, think more positively, or outwork systems that are quietly draining you. It also does not ask you to reject society, escape responsibility, or pretend structure doesn't matter. What it offers instead is a missing layer: **awareness of how modern life actually operates on a human level**.

This is a borderless, culture-neutral book because the problem is not cultural—it is structural. Across countries, economies, and backgrounds, people report the same quiet strain: constant effort with diminishing returns, emotional depletion without clear cause, financial pressure that feels moralized rather than practical. The language may differ. The systems may vary. The exhaustion is the same.

The goal of this book is not to tell you who to blame. Blame drains energy and solves nothing. The goal is to restore orientation.

When you understand *why* things feel harder than they should, you stop internalizing the pressure as personal failure. When you can see the systems clearly, you regain choice. And when you regain choice, sustainability becomes possible again.

Throughout this book, you will not find rigid rules or universal prescriptions. You will find frameworks—simple, adaptable ways to think about money, energy, time, boundaries, and self-respect in a world that quietly extracts all five. These frameworks are not about becoming exceptional. They are about becoming **stable**.

Stability is underrated. Stability is power. Stability is the foundation from which clarity, creativity, and growth naturally emerge.

This book is for people who are functioning but tired. Responsible but stretched thin. Capable yet constantly behind. It is for those who sense that the problem is not laziness or lack of intelligence—but misalignment between human limits and modern expectations.

You do not need to be fixed.

You need to be informed.

Nobody Taught Us This exists to fill the gap—without shame, without ideology, and without telling you who you are supposed to become. It simply offers what was missing: a way to understand how money, energy, and self-respect interact in real life, and how to work with them instead of against yourself.

If modern life has felt harder than it should, this book will show you why.

And once you can see it clearly, you can finally start living in a way that makes sense again.

Chapter 1: Why Smart People Still Struggle

Intelligence Was Never the Missing Piece

Smart people are often told—directly or indirectly—that intelligence should guarantee stability. If you can think clearly, analyze patterns, and learn quickly, life is supposed to cooperate. When it doesn't, the confusion cuts deeper. The struggle feels personal, as if something fundamental has gone wrong.

But intelligence evolved to solve problems, not to navigate invisible systems. Modern life is built on layers of abstraction—financial instruments, social contracts, emotional expectations—that reward compliance and endurance more than understanding. Intelligence alone does not confer immunity to these forces.

In fact, intelligence can increase friction. Smart people notice inconsistencies earlier. They see inefficiencies, contradictions, and quiet unfairness long before others articulate them. That awareness, without instruction, often turns inward as self-doubt rather than outward as system-level critique.

Many intelligent people are trained to internalize responsibility without being taught leverage. They assume that if something isn't working, they must not be trying hard enough or optimizing correctly. The idea that the system itself might be poorly designed rarely enters the equation.

Struggle, then, is not evidence of inadequacy. It is often evidence of perception operating without a map.

The Energy Economy No One Names

Every life operates on an energy budget, but few are taught to track it. Time is measured. Money is counted. Energy—mental, emotional, physical—is assumed to be infinite until it collapses. Smart people often push hardest precisely because they can.

Modern systems quietly reward overextension. Responsiveness is praised. Availability is expected. Burnout is reframed as a personal weakness rather than a predictable outcome. Those who manage complexity well are often given more of it, not less.

Without a language for energy, smart people misattribute exhaustion. They blame motivation, discipline, or mindset when the real issue is leakage—constant, unacknowledged drains from obligations, noise, social friction, and decision overload.

This creates a paradox: the more capable you are, the more invisible labor you absorb. You become the buffer for dysfunction—at work, in families, in systems—until your internal reserves erode.

Energy depletion is not laziness. It is unaccounted expenditure.

Money as a Moral System Instead of a Tool

Money is rarely taught as a neutral system. Instead, it is moralized early: earning equals virtue, struggling equals failure, and wealth implies intelligence or effort. Smart people internalize these narratives deeply, especially when outcomes don't match effort.

But money is not a reflection of worth. It is a set of rules, incentives, bottlenecks, and timing variables. Those rules are complex, often opaque, and frequently misaligned with human rhythms. Intelligence does not automatically reveal them.

Many intelligent individuals follow instructions well: get educated, work hard, be responsible. When the promised stability fails to materialize, the gap feels like betrayal—yet the betrayal is structural, not personal.

Without understanding money as a system, smart people over-identify with outcomes. A bad month becomes a character flaw. A slow year becomes a verdict. This emotional fusion drains clarity and compounds stress.

Money works best when it is understood functionally, not morally.

Social Rules That Reward Silence Over Clarity

From an early age, most people learn that fitting in matters more than making sense. Questioning unspoken rules carries social risk. Smart people notice this quickly and often adapt by self-editing.

They learn when not to speak, when to soften insight, when to absorb discomfort to preserve harmony. Over time, this creates internal dissonance: knowing something is off but lacking permission to address it.

Modern environments amplify this tension. Workplaces, institutions, and even relationships often prioritize smoothness over truth. Those who can see structural issues are subtly discouraged from naming them.

The result is a quiet compression of insight. Intelligence is present, but expression is constrained. That suppression costs energy and breeds frustration without a clear outlet.

Struggle emerges not from ignorance, but from insight without permission.

Responsibility Without Instruction

Responsibility is assigned early and often. Be accountable. Be reliable. Be mature. What is rarely provided is instruction on how to carry responsibility sustainably.

Smart people tend to accept responsibility reflexively. They become problem-solvers by default. When something breaks, they step in—not because they caused it, but because they can handle it.

Over time, this creates imbalance. Responsibility accumulates faster than authority, rest, or compensation. The individual becomes the stabilizing force while remaining structurally unsupported.

This dynamic is exhausting precisely because it feels invisible. Others may praise reliability while continuing to offload weight. The smart person becomes essential and depleted at the same time.

Responsibility without boundaries is not virtue. It is a slow drain.

The Myth of Personal Failure

When systems are invisible, outcomes feel personal. Smart people replay decisions endlessly, searching for the mistake that explains the strain. They assume there must be a smarter way they missed.

But many struggles persist not because of poor choices, but because the environment extracts more than it returns. No amount of optimization can compensate for constant asymmetry.

The myth of personal failure thrives in silence. Without shared language for systemic pressure, individuals shoulder blame that does not belong to them. Intelligence becomes a liability, amplifying self-critique.

Understanding this reframes struggle. It shifts the question from "What is wrong with me?" to "What am I operating inside of?"

That shift restores dignity—and choice.

Framework: The Invisible Load Model

This framework explains why capable people still struggle.

1. **Cognitive Load** – The mental effort of constant decisions, planning, and vigilance
2. **Emotional Load** – Unspoken regulation of others' feelings, expectations, and reactions
3. **Systemic Load** – Navigating rules, costs, and constraints that are poorly explained
4. **Moral Load** – Internalized guilt tied to productivity, money, and rest
5. **Temporal Load** – Living at a pace misaligned with human recovery cycles

Struggle increases when these loads accumulate without acknowledgment or relief.

Quiet Recalibration

This week, notice where effort is being spent without recognition or return. Do not fix it yet. Simply observe. Awareness is the first form of relief.

Reflections

1. Intelligence does not equal insulation from poorly designed systems
2. Energy is spent long before it is noticed
3. Money confusion often hides moral conditioning
4. Silence is frequently a learned survival strategy
5. Responsibility accumulates faster than support

Journal Prompts

1. Where do I assume struggle means personal failure?
2. What drains my energy that I rarely name?
3. How was money framed in my early life?
4. Where do I self-edit to maintain peace?
5. What responsibilities did I inherit without instruction?
6. When did I first feel “behind” despite effort?
7. What systems do I operate in without understanding their rules?
8. How do I measure my worth day to day?
9. Where am I reliable at my own expense?
10. What would change if struggle were not a verdict on me?

Closing Reflection

Smart people do not struggle because they lack insight. They struggle because insight alone cannot compensate for invisible systems, unspoken rules, and unacknowledged load. When the environment is unclear, intelligence turns inward and becomes self-criticism. This chapter is not an excuse—it is a reorientation. Once you can see the forces at play, you stop fighting yourself and start choosing where your effort truly belongs.

Chapter 2: Money Stress Is Emotional First

Money Activates the Nervous System Before the Calculator

Most people believe money problems are numerical. Not enough income. Too many expenses. Bad budgeting. Poor planning. But long before math enters the picture, the nervous system reacts. Tightness. Urgency. Shame. Fear. Those reactions shape decisions faster than logic ever could.

Money conversations trigger survival wiring because money represents access: to safety, food, shelter, status, and time. When access feels threatened, the body responds as if danger is present—even when the threat is abstract or delayed. This is why calm financial advice often fails under stress.

Smart people are especially vulnerable here. They assume understanding numbers should neutralize anxiety. When it doesn't, they interpret the emotional response as weakness rather than biology. That misinterpretation deepens the spiral.

Under stress, the brain prioritizes short-term relief over long-term optimization. This is not stupidity. It is survival logic misapplied to modern systems. The math doesn't fail—the context does.

Until emotional activation is addressed, financial clarity remains out of reach.

Fear Shrinks Time Horizons

Fear collapses perspective. When money feels scarce, the future contracts. Decisions become reactive: pay this now, avoid that consequence, relieve this pressure. Long-term thinking feels inaccessible, not because it's unknown, but because it feels unsafe.

This is why people make choices they later regret while fully understanding the consequences at the time. Fear does not erase knowledge—it overrides it. The goal becomes reducing discomfort, not maximizing outcome.

Financial advice often assumes a calm decision-maker with stable bandwidth. In reality, most financial decisions are made under emotional compression: deadlines, threats, judgment, or uncertainty. The system then punishes the very reactions it provokes.

Smart people often blame themselves for "knowing better." But knowing better does not deactivate fear. It only increases shame when fear wins.

Money stress is not ignorance. It is time pressure amplified by emotion.

Shame Is the Hidden Interest Rate

Shame quietly compounds every financial challenge. It discourages asking questions, delays action, and isolates people when support would help most. Unlike fees or interest, shame is invisible—but far more expensive.

From early life, money is framed as a character test. Success implies responsibility. Struggle implies failure. These narratives attach identity to outcome, making neutral problem-solving emotionally dangerous.

When shame enters the equation, avoidance follows. Bills go unopened. Accounts go unchecked. Conversations are postponed. The issue grows—not because of denial, but because of emotional pain associated with attention.

Smart people often hide money stress better than others. They compensate socially, intellectually, or creatively while pressure builds privately. The silence preserves image at the cost of clarity.

Shame does not motivate improvement. It delays it.

Scarcity Thinking Distorts Reality

Scarcity is not just having less—it is thinking under conditions of "never enough." When scarcity dominates, every decision feels loaded. Spending feels risky. Saving feels insufficient. Earning feels fragile.

This mindset narrows options. People over-focus on immediate numbers while missing structural patterns. They optimize small decisions while remaining trapped in larger constraints.

Scarcity thinking also distorts self-perception. Effort feels invisible. Progress feels erased. Gains feel temporary. Losses feel permanent. None of this reflects reality—it reflects nervous system bias under threat.

Financial systems often intensify scarcity by design: variable income, unpredictable costs, delayed rewards. The individual absorbs the volatility emotionally, even when the math fluctuates normally.

Scarcity is not a personality flaw. It is a condition—and conditions can change.

Why Advice Rarely Matches Lived Reality

Most financial advice assumes emotional neutrality. Create a budget. Cut expenses. Increase income. These steps are not wrong—but they ignore the state of the person expected to implement them.

Advice that bypasses fear often feels dismissive. Advice that ignores shame feels unrealistic. Advice that overlooks energy feels impossible. As a result, people disengage—not because they reject logic, but because the logic doesn't meet them where they are.

Smart people may consume large amounts of financial information without applying it. This creates a false narrative of irresponsibility. In reality, the missing step is emotional regulation, not education.

Money decisions improve when the nervous system stabilizes first. Only then does math regain relevance.

Clarity follows safety, not the other way around.

Reframing Control Without Blame

Control is often misunderstood as strict discipline. In money matters, real control begins with emotional literacy—recognizing what state you are in before deciding anything.

This reframing removes moral judgment. Fear is not failure. Avoidance is not laziness. Overreaction is not stupidity. These are signals, not verdicts.

When emotion is acknowledged, choice expands. People pause. They slow decisions. They separate identity from outcome. This alone reduces costly mistakes.

Smart people regain leverage not by suppressing emotion, but by working with it consciously. Emotional awareness becomes a financial skill.

Money becomes manageable again when it stops feeling like a threat to identity.

Framework: The Emotional-First Money Loop

This framework explains why financial stress persists despite intelligence.

1. **Trigger** – A bill, deadline, comparison, or uncertainty activates fear
2. **Emotional Response** – Anxiety, shame, urgency, or dread emerges
3. **Behavior** – Avoidance, impulsive action, overcontrol, or shutdown
4. **Outcome** – Temporary relief or compounded stress
5. **Narrative** – Self-blame replaces system awareness

Breaking the loop requires intervening at the emotional stage—not the math stage.

Quiet Recalibration

Before your next financial decision, pause for one full minute. Name what you feel without fixing it. Decisions made after acknowledgment carry less hidden cost.

Reflections

1. Money stress often begins in the body, not the spreadsheet
2. Fear shortens time horizons and narrows choice
3. Shame quietly delays solvable problems
4. Scarcity thinking distorts perception more than numbers do
5. Emotional awareness restores financial agency

Journal Prompts

1. What emotions arise when I think about money right now?
2. When did money first feel tied to my worth?
3. What financial situations trigger urgency or avoidance in me?
4. How do I behave differently under money stress?
5. Where has shame delayed action in my financial life?
6. What decisions do I regret that were fear-driven?
7. How does scarcity thinking show up in my daily choices?
8. What financial advice have I ignored—and why?
9. How does my body react to money conversations?
10. What would change if money were emotionally neutral?

Closing Reflection

Money feels mathematical, but it is processed emotionally first. Fear, shame, and scarcity shape decisions long before logic is consulted. This does not mean people are irrational—it means they are human. When emotional pressure is mistaken for personal failure, stress multiplies. When it is recognized as the starting point, clarity returns. Financial stability begins not with better math, but with calmer ground to stand on.

Chapter 3: Boundaries Are a Survival Skill

Boundaries Protect Life Before They Protect Comfort

Boundaries are often framed as a social preference—something you set once you feel confident or secure. In reality, boundaries are a biological necessity. They regulate exposure to stress, demand, and depletion long before questions of politeness or self-expression arise.

Every system that sustains life has limits. Cells have membranes. Ecosystems have carrying capacity. Bodies require rest. Humans are no different, yet we are rarely taught to treat limits as non-negotiable.

Instead, limits are portrayed as negotiable traits. Being flexible is praised. Being available is rewarded. Saying yes is framed as maturity, while saying no is associated with selfishness or weakness. This inversion quietly trains people to override their own warning signals.

Smart, capable people often last longer without boundaries, which makes the eventual collapse more confusing. They don't fail suddenly—they erode slowly.

Boundaries are not about control. They are about survival over time.

Why No Feels Dangerous Even When It Isn't

For many people, saying no triggers disproportionate fear. Fear of conflict. Fear of rejection. Fear of being misunderstood or abandoned. This fear rarely comes from the present moment—it is inherited from earlier environments.

In childhood and early social conditioning, approval often depended on compliance. Needs were rewarded when convenient. Discomfort was tolerated to preserve harmony. Over time, saying no became associated with risk rather than safety.

Modern systems amplify this conditioning. Workplaces, institutions, and families often operate on implied obligation rather than explicit agreement. Saying no threatens the unspoken contract: if you are capable, you will absorb the extra load.

Smart people internalize this quickly. They anticipate consequences before they happen. They preemptively comply to avoid friction. What looks like generosity is often threat avoidance.

The danger was real once. The habit remained long after.

Boundary Failure Looks Like Burnout, Not Rebellion

When boundaries fail, the result is rarely dramatic refusal. It is quiet depletion. Chronic fatigue. Irritability without a clear cause. Loss of creativity. Emotional numbness. These are not personality changes—they are symptoms.

Without boundaries, life becomes reactive. Priorities are dictated by whoever speaks loudest or needs most urgently. Time fragments. Recovery disappears. The individual remains functional but drained.

Because boundary failure is invisible, it is often misdiagnosed. People assume they need better discipline, motivation, or mindset. They push harder into an already depleted system.

Smart people are especially vulnerable because they can compensate longer. They optimize. They adapt. They endure. Endurance is mistaken for resilience until the cost becomes unavoidable.

Burnout is not a failure of strength. It is a failure of limits.

Boundaries Are Clarity, Not Confrontation

Many people avoid boundaries because they associate them with conflict. They imagine raised voices, ultimatums, or emotional fallout. In reality, most boundaries do not require explanation, justification, or confrontation.

A boundary is simply a clear internal decision about what you will and will not sustain. External communication comes later—and often less dramatically than expected.

The absence of boundaries creates far more conflict than their presence. Resentment accumulates. Expectations go unspoken. Relationships strain under unacknowledged imbalance.

Clarity reduces friction. When limits are consistent, others adapt. When limits are absent, confusion reigns. The chaos that follows is often blamed on personalities rather than structure.

Boundaries simplify life by reducing negotiation at the wrong level.

Why Saying Yes Too Often Is a Systemic Risk

Every yes has a cost, even when it feels small. Time spent cannot be recovered. Energy expended must be replenished. Attention given elsewhere is attention not given to recovery or growth.

Systems rely on unbounded individuals to remain stable. When someone absorbs extra work, emotional labor, or responsibility without resistance, the system has no incentive to change.

Smart people become the shock absorbers of dysfunction. Their reliability hides the problem. Their silence normalizes overload. Over time, they carry weight that was never meant to be personal.

Saying no is not withdrawal—it is correction. It exposes imbalance so it can be addressed where it belongs.

Without no, systems drift toward extraction.

Learning Boundaries Without Becoming Hard

There is a fear that boundaries will make someone cold, rigid, or unkind. This fear is rooted in a false choice between self-protection and connection.

Healthy boundaries do not eliminate generosity. They preserve it. When energy is protected, giving becomes intentional rather than compulsory. Kindness becomes sustainable rather than draining.

Boundaries allow presence. They prevent resentment. They make rest possible without guilt. Over time, they restore trust in one's own signals.

Smart people often soften boundaries to avoid harm. But unprotected softness becomes erosion. Strength without boundaries is brittle.

Boundaries do not harden you. They stabilize you.

Framework: The Boundary Load Filter

Use this framework to decide when no is necessary.

1. **Capacity** – Do I have the energy to sustain this without recovery debt?
2. **Consent** – Did I freely choose this, or did I default into it?
3. **Cost** – What will this displace or delay?
4. **Continuity** – If this became normal, could I survive it long-term?
5. **Correction** – Is this covering a system problem that needs visibility?

If three or more raise concern, a boundary is required.

Quiet Recalibration

For the next request you receive, pause before responding. Ask yourself whether your yes would be chosen or automatic. Choose deliberately.

Reflections

1. Boundaries preserve energy before they preserve comfort
2. Fear around no is often inherited, not current
3. Burnout signals missing limits, not missing strength
4. Clarity reduces conflict more than compliance does
5. Saying no corrects systems, not relationships

Journal Prompts

1. Where do I say yes to avoid discomfort rather than agreement?
2. What happens in my body when I consider saying no?
3. Which responsibilities did I never consciously choose?
4. Where has reliability become a liability?
5. What boundary would immediately reduce my exhaustion?
6. Who benefits most from my lack of limits?
7. What do I fear would happen if I said no more often?
8. Where do I confuse kindness with endurance?
9. How do I recover after giving—if at all?
10. What would sustainable generosity look like for me?

Closing Reflection

Boundaries are not an advanced skill reserved for confident or confrontational people. They are a foundational survival tool in a world that quietly extracts from the capable and the conscientious. Saying no is not rejection—it is regulation. When limits are restored, energy stabilizes, clarity returns, and life becomes navigable again. Boundaries do not reduce what you can give. They ensure you remain alive enough to give at all.

Chapter 4: The Cost of Carrying Everyone Else

Over-Responsibility Is Learned, Not Chosen

Most people who carry too much did not volunteer for the role. They adapted into it. Somewhere early, they learned that stability depended on them staying alert, useful, and composed. When chaos appeared, they stepped in—not because it was fair, but because it worked.

Over time, this adaptation hardened into identity. The reliable one. The fixer. The calm one. The one who "can handle it." What began as survival slowly became expectation—both from others and from the self.

Over-responsibility is often praised. It looks like maturity, leadership, and strength. But praise conceals the cost. No one asks how much capacity is being spent to maintain that image.

Smart, capable people rarely notice the transition point where help turns into burden. Responsibility accumulates quietly, layer by layer, until stepping back feels impossible.

What looks like character is often conditioning reinforced by necessity.

The Body Pays First, Even When the Mind Keeps Going

The body registers overload long before the mind admits it. Tension becomes constant. Sleep becomes shallow. Focus fragments. Small tasks feel heavier than they should. These are not random symptoms—they are signals.

When someone carries responsibility that exceeds their recovery capacity, the nervous system stays partially activated at all times. The body never fully exits readiness mode. This drains health invisibly, day after day.

Smart people override these signals because they can still perform. They mistake functionality for sustainability. As long as output continues, warning signs are minimized or ignored.

Eventually, the cost surfaces as illness, chronic pain, anxiety, or collapse—but by then the load feels irreversible. The body didn't fail. It endured until it couldn't.

Health erosion is often deferred payment for long-term overextension.

Focus Deteriorates Under Invisible Load

Over-responsibility fractures attention. The mind becomes a background task manager, constantly tracking obligations, risks, and contingencies. Even during rest, part of the brain remains on duty.

This reduces depth. Creative thought suffers. Long-term planning becomes difficult. The mind jumps between concerns instead of settling into clarity. People often misinterpret this as distraction or decline in ability.

In reality, focus is being consumed by unacknowledged labor. Worry, anticipation, emotional regulation, and problem prevention all take cognitive resources—even when nothing is actively happening.

Smart people often respond by pushing harder: more systems, more discipline, more optimization. But focus cannot be forced when bandwidth is already saturated.

Attention returns when the load is reduced, not when effort increases.

Why Letting Go Feels Like Threat

Releasing responsibility often triggers fear disproportionate to the task itself. Fear that things will fall apart. Fear of being judged. Fear of becoming unnecessary or replaceable.

These fears are rarely about the present situation. They are echoes of earlier environments where withdrawal meant loss—of safety, approval, or belonging. Responsibility became the price of security.

Modern systems exploit this conditioning. Those who carry more are given more. Those who don't complain are relied upon most. Over time, the individual becomes essential but unsupported.

Letting go feels dangerous because the system has adjusted around your sacrifice. That does not make the sacrifice healthy.

Responsibility that cannot be set down is no longer responsibility—it is entrapment.

The Illusion of Control Through Carrying

Many over-responsible people believe carrying everything keeps chaos contained. If they stay vigilant, problems won't escalate. If they manage everyone else's needs, things will remain stable.

This belief creates an illusion of control that feels safer than uncertainty. But it comes at a high cost: constant vigilance, emotional suppression, and personal neglect.

Carrying does not prevent chaos—it postpones it by internalizing the damage. The system appears stable while one person absorbs the strain.

Eventually, control collapses not because the person failed, but because the load exceeded human limits. The fallout feels personal, even though it was structural.

True stability distributes weight. It does not hide it inside one person.

Reclaiming Self Without Abandoning Others

The fear underlying over-responsibility is often moral: if I stop carrying, I am selfish. If I rest, others will suffer. If I focus on myself, I am abandoning people.

This is a false binary. Reducing over-responsibility does not require cruelty or indifference. It requires redefining what is truly yours to carry.

Healthy responsibility has edges. It includes choice, consent, and recovery. When those are restored, support becomes sustainable rather than sacrificial.

Smart people do not need to become harder. They need to become more accurate about where their responsibility ends.

Care that destroys the caregiver is not care—it is slow self-erasure.

Framework: The Responsibility Load Audit

Use this framework to identify hidden overload.

1. **Origin** – Did I choose this responsibility, or did it default to me?
2. **Authority** – Do I have real power to shape outcomes here?
3. **Recovery** – Is there time or space to replenish what this takes?
4. **Visibility** – Is this labor acknowledged or invisible?
5. **Replaceability** – Would this truly collapse if I stepped back?

If responsibility lacks authority, recovery, or visibility, it is likely overextended.

Quiet Recalibration

This week, identify one responsibility you could pause, delegate, or soften without catastrophe. Observe what actually happens—not what you fear will happen.

Reflections

1. Over-responsibility is often inherited through adaptation
2. The body absorbs overload before the mind admits it
3. Focus fractures under unacknowledged cognitive labor
4. Letting go feels threatening when identity is tied to carrying
5. Stability should distribute weight, not conceal it

Journal Prompts

1. What am I carrying that no one explicitly asked me to carry?
2. Where has responsibility replaced rest in my life?
3. How does my body signal overload?
4. What do I fear would happen if I stepped back slightly?
5. Which responsibilities drain me without giving authority?
6. Where do I equate usefulness with worth?
7. What would collapse—and what would adapt—if I carried less?
8. How does over-responsibility affect my focus and creativity?
9. Who benefits most from my constant availability?
10. What would sustainable responsibility look like for me?

Closing Reflection

Carrying everyone else does not make you strong—it makes you depleted. Over-responsibility quietly erodes health, fragments focus, and binds identity to endurance. This chapter is not an instruction to abandon care, but an invitation to redistribute weight. When responsibility becomes intentional instead of automatic, clarity returns. You do not lose your value by carrying less. You regain your life.

Chapter 5: Building a Life That Doesn't Collapse Under Pressure

Stability Is Not the Absence of Stress

Many people believe stability means eliminating pressure. A calm schedule. Predictable income. Minimal disruption. But modern life makes total calm unrealistic. Pressure is not the anomaly—it is the environment.

Stability, then, cannot depend on perfect conditions. It must function *within* disruption. A life that only works when nothing goes wrong is fragile by design.

Smart people often build systems optimized for best-case scenarios. When those scenarios fail—as they inevitably do—the entire structure buckles. The collapse feels sudden, but the vulnerability was always there.

True stability is not about controlling the world. It is about designing yourself and your systems to bend without breaking.

A stable life is one that degrades gracefully instead of catastrophically.

Redundancy Is Strength, Not Waste

Modern efficiency culture treats redundancy as inefficiency. Backup plans look pessimistic. Slack looks lazy. Extra capacity looks unnecessary—until it is the only thing standing between continuity and collapse.

Biological systems rely on redundancy to survive. Multiple pathways. Reserve energy. Overlapping functions. Human lives are no different, yet we are taught to run at maximum utilization.

Smart people often eliminate redundancy to appear competent. They schedule tightly, budget narrowly, and rely on single points of failure—one income stream, one caretaker, one role, one identity.

When disruption hits, there is nowhere to absorb it. Stress spikes because the system has no buffer.

Redundancy is not excess. It is insurance against reality.

Stability Begins With Energy Before Strategy

Most life plans focus on strategy: goals, timelines, metrics, and milestones. But strategy collapses without energy to execute it. Exhausted people cannot maintain even the best plans.

Energy determines resilience. When energy is stable, decisions improve. Recovery accelerates. Perspective widens. When energy is unstable, everything feels urgent and fragile.

Smart people often treat energy as secondary because it feels subjective. They track tasks but not depletion. They measure output but not recovery.

A stable life tracks energy as a primary variable. It designs days, obligations, and goals around sustainable output rather than maximum performance.

Strategy follows energy, not the other way around.

Pressure Reveals Structure, Not Character

Under pressure, people often believe they are seeing their true selves. If they panic, freeze, or make mistakes, they interpret it as a personal flaw. In reality, pressure reveals system design.

A well-structured life absorbs shocks. A poorly structured one transfers stress directly into the body and mind. The response feels personal, but the cause is architectural.

Smart people internalize breakdowns because they assume competence should compensate for design flaws. They blame themselves instead of examining the load path.

When pressure hits, ask not "What is wrong with me?" but "What is this pressure traveling through?"

Redesign begins with structure, not self-criticism.

Optionality Is the Core of Modern Security

In uncertain times, certainty is rare—but options create stability. Optionality means having more than one viable path when conditions change.

This applies to money, time, relationships, identity, and location. The more singular your dependency, the more pressure concentrates there.

Smart people often specialize deeply and depend heavily on narrow systems. This creates excellence—but also fragility. When the system shifts, adaptation becomes painful.

Optionality does not require abandoning commitment. It requires maintaining flexibility within commitment.

Security today is not permanence. It is the ability to pivot without collapse.

A Stable Life Is Quiet, Not Performative

Modern culture rewards visible success: productivity, hustle, constant improvement. Stability, by contrast, is subtle. It looks like fewer emergencies, calmer responses, and consistent functioning.

Because it lacks drama, stability is undervalued. People chase intensity thinking it equals progress. Over time, intensity without structure leads to burnout.

Smart people may feel uneasy when life becomes quiet. The absence of pressure feels unfamiliar, even suspicious. They mistake calm for stagnation.

But quiet systems last. They free attention for creativity, depth, and meaning rather than constant repair.

A life that doesn't collapse rarely announces itself. It simply keeps going.

Framework: The Stability Stack

This framework outlines the layers of a pressure-resistant life.

1. **Energy Floor** – Minimum rest, recovery, and health required to function
2. **Load Limits** – Clear caps on responsibility, obligation, and output
3. **Redundancy** – Buffers in money, time, and support systems
4. **Optionality** – Multiple viable paths when conditions change
5. **Recovery Loops** – Regular cycles that restore capacity before depletion

Weakness at any layer increases collapse risk under stress.

Quiet Recalibration

Choose one area of life where you are operating without buffer. Add a small margin—not to optimize, but to stabilize.

Reflections

1. Stability must function under pressure, not avoid it
2. Redundancy prevents collapse more than efficiency does
3. Energy determines whether strategy survives reality
4. Pressure exposes structure, not personal worth
5. Quiet systems outlast dramatic ones

Journal Prompts

1. Where does my life rely on best-case assumptions?
2. What single point of failure creates the most stress for me?
3. How do I currently track—or ignore—my energy levels?
4. Where would redundancy immediately reduce anxiety?
5. What pressure repeatedly overwhelms my systems?
6. How many viable options do I have in key areas of life?
7. Where do I confuse intensity with progress?
8. What does stability look like in my daily experience?
9. How does my life behave when something goes wrong?
10. What would I redesign if collapse were not an option?

Closing Reflection

A life that doesn't collapse under pressure is not built through force or perfection. It is built through design. Stability comes from honoring limits, preserving energy, creating buffers, and maintaining options in an uncertain world. This chapter is not about predicting the future—it is about becoming resilient enough to meet it. When life is structured to absorb stress instead of amplifying it, pressure loses its power. What remains is continuity, clarity, and the quiet confidence that you can endure without breaking.

Appendix A: The Human Basics Checklist

What This Checklist Is—and What It Is Not

This checklist is not a productivity system, a self-optimization protocol, or a moral scorecard. It is a **stability check**—a way to verify that the fundamentals of being human are being met before asking yourself to perform, improve, or endure more.

Most breakdowns do not begin with dramatic failures. They begin with neglected basics: sleep eroding quietly, energy leaking unnoticed, boundaries thinning, money stress activating fear, and responsibility accumulating without relief. This checklist exists to interrupt that drift.

Revisit it **once per season**. Not daily. Not obsessively. Seasonal review creates distance, perspective, and honesty without turning self-awareness into pressure.

The goal is not perfection.
The goal is **early correction**.

1. Body & Energy Fundamentals

◈ I am getting enough sleep to feel mentally clear most days
◈ My body has predictable access to food and hydration
◈ I have at least one low-stimulation period each day
◈ Pain, tension, or fatigue is acknowledged rather than ignored
◈ I am not relying on constant adrenaline to function

Seasonal Check:

If energy feels lower than last season, identify *what increased*—not what you failed to do.

2. Nervous System & Emotional Load

◈ I experience moments of calm without guilt
◈ My life includes emotional recovery, not just endurance
◈ I am not constantly bracing for the next problem
◈ I can name what I'm feeling without immediately fixing it
◈ Emotional labor is shared, not silently absorbed

Seasonal Check:

Notice whether stress feels sharper, flatter, or heavier than before. Each signals a different kind of overload.

3. Money & Material Stability

⯑ I know my basic monthly numbers (income, essentials, margin)
⯑ Money stress is named without self-judgment
⯑ I am not avoiding financial information out of fear or shame
⯑ My survival does not depend on constant urgency
⯑ I have at least one small buffer, even if imperfect

Seasonal Check:

Ask whether money feels like a threat, a tool, or a constant background noise—and whether that has shifted.

4. Boundaries & Capacity

◈ I know what I can realistically sustain right now
◈ I say no without explaining myself excessively
◈ I am not defaulting into responsibility without consent
◈ Rest is allowed before collapse, not after
◈ My availability has limits I respect

Seasonal Check:

Identify one boundary that softened unintentionally and decide whether it needs to be restored.

5. Responsibility & Load Distribution

◈ I am not carrying roles that belong to systems or others
◈ Responsibility comes with authority or choice
◈ I have permission to step back without guilt
◈ My usefulness is not my only value
◈ I am allowed to be supported

Seasonal Check:

Notice whether responsibility feels heavier or more automatic than last season.

6. Focus, Attention, & Cognitive Space

◈ I can concentrate without constant interruption
◈ My mind has space for depth, not just reaction
◈ I am not multitasking my way through life
◈ Worry is not occupying background attention all day
◈ I experience moments of mental quiet

Seasonal Check:

If focus has declined, look for added load—not missing discipline.

7. Social & Environmental Safety

◈ My environment feels mostly predictable and non-threatening
◈ I am not constantly managing others' emotions
◈ I have at least one space where I can be unguarded
◈ Conflict is not my default state
◈ I feel allowed to exist without performing

Seasonal Check:

Ask whether your environment has become louder, faster, or more demanding—and how that affects you.

8. Meaning & Direction (Without Pressure)

◇ My life feels coherent, even if unfinished
◇ I am not chasing goals to escape discomfort
◇ Progress is defined by stability, not speed
◇ I know what matters *this season*
◇ I am allowed to pause without losing identity

Seasonal Check:
Direction can change without failure. Ask what matters *now*, not forever.

How to Use This Checklist

- Review it **four times a year**
- Answer honestly, not optimistically
- Do not fix everything—choose **one area** per season
- Track trends, not moments
- Treat decline as information, not judgment

Stability improves through **small, timely corrections**, not dramatic resets.

Seasonal Reflection Questions

1. What feels heavier than last season—and why?
2. What quietly improved without effort?
3. Where did I override my limits most often?
4. What support did I need but not request?
5. What would make the next season gentler without reducing responsibility?

Journal Prompts

1. Which basics have I been postponing?
2. What does my body need more of right now?
3. Where am I confusing endurance with strength?
4. What pressure feels unnecessary in hindsight?
5. What boundary would restore the most energy?
6. How does money stress show up emotionally for me?
7. What responsibility no longer belongs to me?
8. Where does my attention leak the most?
9. What does stability actually feel like in my body?
10. What would "enough" look like this season?

Closing Reflection

Most people do not struggle because they are unmotivated or incapable. They struggle because the fundamentals of being human are quietly violated over time. This checklist is not about becoming more—it is about maintaining *enough*. When the basics are protected, clarity returns. Focus stabilizes. Decisions improve. Life stops feeling like a constant emergency. Revisit these questions season by season, not to judge yourself, but to stay oriented. A stable human foundation is not a luxury. It is the condition that makes everything else possible.

Message from the Author:

I hope you enjoyed this book, I love astrology and knew there was not a book such as this out on the shelf. I love metaphysical items as well. Please check out my other books:

-Life of Government Benefits

-My life of Hell

-My life with Hydrocephalus

-Red Sky

-World Domination:Woman's rule

-World Domination:Woman's Rule 2: The War

-Life and Banishment of Apophis: book 1

-The Kidney Friendly Diet

-The Ultimate Hemp Cookbook

-Creating a Dispensary(legally)

-Cleanliness throughout life: the importance of showering from childhood to adulthood.

-Strong Roots: The Risks of Overcoddling children

-Hemp Horoscopes: Cosmic Insights and Earthly Healing

- Celestial Hemp Navigating the Zodiac: Through the Green Cosmos

-Astrological Hemp: Aligning The Stars with Earth's Ancient Herb

-The Astrological Guide to Hemp: Stars, Signs, and Sacred Leaves

-Green Growth: Innovative Marketing Strategies for your Hemp Products and Dispensary

-Cosmic Cannabis

-Astrological Munchies

-Henry The Hemp

-Zodiacal Roots: The Astrological Soul Of Hemp

- **Green Constellations: Intersection of Hemp and Zodiac**

-Hemp in The Houses: An astrological Adventure Through The Cannabis Galaxy

-Galactic Ganja Guide

Heavenly Hemp

Zodiac Leaves

Doctor Who Astrology

Cannastrology

Stellar Satvias and Cosmic Indicas

Celestial Cannabis: A Zodiac Journey

AstroHerbology: The Sky and The Soil: Volume 1

AstroHerbology:Celestial Cannabis:Volume 2

Cosmic Cannabis Cultivation

The Starry Guide to Herbal Harmony: Volume 1

The Starry Guide to Herbal Harmony: Cannabis Universe: Volume 2

Yugioh Astrology: Astrological Guide to Deck, Duels and more

Nightmare Mansion: Echoes of The Abyss

Nightmare Mansion 2: Legacy of Shadows

Nightmare Mansion 3: Shadows of the Forgotten

Nightmare Mansion 4: Echoes of the Damned

The Life and Banishment of Apophis: Book 2

Nightmare Mansion: Halls of Despair

Healing with Herb: Cannabis and Hydrocephalus

Planetary Pot: Aligning with Astrological Herbs: Volume 1

Fast Track to Freedom: 30 Days to Financial Independence Using AI, Assets, and Agile Hustles

Cosmic Hemp Pathways

How to Become Financially Free in 30 Days: 10,000 Paths to Prosperity

Zodiacal Herbage: Astrological Insights: Volume 1

Nightmare Mansion: Whispers in the Walls

The Daleks Invade Atlantis

Henry the hemp and Hydrocephalus

10X The Kidney Friendly Diet

Cannabis Universe: Adult coloring book

Hemp Astrology: The Healing Power of the Stars

Zodiacal Herbage: Astrological Insights: Cannabis Universe: Volume 2

Planetary Pot: Aligning with Astrological Herbs: Cannabis Universes: Volume 2

Doctor Who: Convergence Protocol – The Replicator War

Nightmare Mansion: Curse of the Blood Moon

The Celestial Stoner: A Guide to the Zodiac

Cosmic Pleasures: Sex Toy Astrology for Every Sign

Hydrocephalus Astrology: Navigating the Stars and Healing Waters

Lapis and the Mischievous Chocolate Bar

Celestial Positions: Sexual Astrology for Every Sign

Apophis's Shadow Work Journal: **:** A Journey of Self-Discovery and Healing

Kinky Cosmos: Sexual Kink Astrology for Every Sign

Digital Cosmos: The Astrological Digimon Compendium

Stellar Seeds: The Cosmic Guide to Growing with Astrology

Apophis's Daily Gratitude Journal

Cat Astrology: Feline Mysteries of the Cosmos

The Cosmic Kama Sutra: An Astrological Guide to Sexual Positions

Unleash Your Potential: A Guided Journal Powered by AI Insights

Whispers of the Enchanted Grove

Cosmic Pleasures: An Astrological Guide to Sexual Kinks

369, 12 Manifestation Journal

Whisper of the nocturne journal(blank journal for writing or drawing)

The Boogey Book

Locked In Reflection: A Chastity Journey Through Locktober

Generating Wealth Quickly:How to Generate $100,000 in 24 Hours

Star Magic: Harness the Power of the Universe

The Flatulence Chronicles: A Fart Journal for Self-Discovery

The Doctor and The Death Moth

Seize the Day: A Personal Seizure Tracking Journal

The Ultimate Boogeyman Safari: A Journey into the Boogie World and Beyond

Whispers of Samhain: 1,000 Spells of Love, Luck, and Lunar Magic: Samhain Spell Book

Apophis's guides:Witch's Spellbook Crafting Guide for Halloween

Frost & Flame: The Enchanted Yule Grimoire of 1000 Winter Spells

The Ultimate Boogey Goo Guide & Spooky Activities for Halloween Fun

Harmony of the Scales: A Libra's Spellcraft for Balance and Beauty

The Enchanted Advent: 36 Days of Christmas Wonders

Nightmare Mansion: The Labyrinth of Screams

Harvest of Enchantment: 1,000 Spells of Gratitude, Love, and Fortune for Thanksgiving

The Boogey Chronicles: A Journal of Nightly Encounters and Shadowy Secrets

The 12 Days of Financial Freedom: A Step-by-Step Christmas Countdown to Transform Your Finances

Sigil of the Eternal Spiral Blank Journal

A Christmas Feast: Timeless Recipes for Every Meal

Holiday Stress-Free Solutions: A Survival Guide to Thriving During the Festive Season

Yu-Gi-Oh! Holiday Gifting Mastery: The Ultimate Guide for Fans and Newcomers Alike

Holiday Harmony: A Hydrocephalus Survival Guide for the Festive Season

Celestial Craft: The Witch's Almanac for 2025 – A Cosmic Guide to Manifestations, Moons, and Mystical Events

Doctor Who: The Toymaker's Winter Wonderland

Tulsa King Unveiled: A Thrilling Guide to Stallone's Mafia Masterpiece

Pendulum Craft: A Complete Guide to Crafting and Using Personalized Divination Tools

Nightmare Mansion: Santa's Eternal Eve

Starlight Noel: A Cosmic Journey through Christmas Mysteries

The Dark Architect: Unlocking the Blueprint of Existence

Surviving the Embrace: The Ultimate Guide to Encounters with The Hugging Molly

The Enchanted Codex: Secrets of the Craft for Witches, Wiccans, and Pagans

Harvest of Gratitude: A Complete Thanksgiving Guide

Yuletide Essentials: A Complete Guide to an Authentic and Magical Christmas

Celestial Smokes: A Cosmic Guide to Cigars and Astrology

Living in Balance: A Comprehensive Survival Guide to Thriving with Diabetes Insipidus

Cosmic Symbiosis: The Venom Zodiac Chronicles

The Cursed Paw of Ambition

Cosmic Symbiosis: The Astrological Venom Journal

Celestial Wonders Unfold: A Stargazer's Guide to the Cosmos (2024-2029)

The Ultimate Black Friday Prepper's Guide: Mastering Shopping Strategies and Savings

Cosmic Sales: The Astrological Guide to Black Friday Shopping

Legends of the Corn Mother and Other Harvest Myths

Whispers of the Harvest: The Corn Mother's Journal
The Evergreen Spellbook
The Doctor Meets the Boogeyman
The White Witch of Rose Hall's SpellBook
The Gingerbread Golem's Shadow: A Study in Sweet Darkness
The Gingerbread Golem Codex: An Academic Exploration of Sweet Myths
The Gingerbread Golem Grimoire: Sweet Magicks and Spells for the Festive Witch
The Curse of the Gingerbread Golem
10-minute Christmas Crafts for kids
Christmas Crisis Solutions: The Ultimate Last-Minute Survival Guide
Gingerbread Golem Recipes: Holiday Treats with a Magical Twist
The Infinite Key: Unlocking Mystical Secrets of the Ages
Enchanted Yule: A Wiccan and Pagan Guide to a Magical and Memorable Season
Dinosaurs of Power: Unlocking Ancient Magick
Astro-Dinos: The Cosmic Guide to Prehistoric Wisdom
Gallifrey's Yule Logs: A Festive Doctor Who Cookbook
The Dino Grimoire: Secrets of Prehistoric Magick
The Gift They Never Knew They Needed
The Gingerbread Golem's Culinary Alchemy: Enchanting Recipes for a Sweetly Dark Feast
A Time Lord Christmas: Holiday Adventures with the Doctor
Krampusproofing Your Home: Defensive Strategies for Yule
Silent Frights: A Collection of Christmas Creepypastas to Chill Your Bones
Santa Raptor's Jolly Carnage: A Dino-Claus Christmas Tale
Prehistoric Palettes: A Dino Wicca Coloring Journey
The Christmas Wishkeeper Chronicles
The Starlight Sleigh: A Holiday Journey
Elf Secrets: The True Magic of the North Pole

Candy Cane Conjurations

Cooking with Kids: Recipes Under 20 Minutes

Doctor Who: The TARDIS Confiscation

The Anxiety First Aid Kit: Quick Tools to Calm Your Mind

Frosty Whispers: A Winter's Tale

The Infinite Key: Unlocking the Secrets to Prosperity, Resilience, and Purpose

The Grasping Void: Why You'll Regret This Purchase

Astrology for Busy Bees: Star Signs Simplified

The Instant Focus Formula: Cut Through the Noise

The Secret Language of Colors: Unlocking the Emotional Codes

Sacred Fossil Chronicles: Blank Journal

The Christmas Cottage Miracle

Feeding Frenzy: Graboid-Inspired Recipes

Manifest in Minutes: The Quick Law of Attraction Guide

The Symbiote Chronicles: Doctor Who's Venomous Journey

Think Tiny, Grow Big: The Minimalist Mindset

The Energy Key: Unlocking Limitless Motivation

New Year, New Magic: Manifesting Your Best Year Yet

Unstoppable You: Mastering Confidence in Minutes

Infinite Energy: The Secret to Never Feeling Drained

Lightning Focus: Mastering the Art of Productivity in a Distracted World

Saturnalia Manifestation Magick: A Guide to Unlocking Abundance During the Solstice

Graboids and Garland: The Ultimate Tremors-Themed Christmas Guide

12 Nights of Holiday Magic

The Power of Pause: 60-Second Mindfulness Practices

The Quick Reset: How to Reclaim Your Life After Burnout

The Shadow Eater: A Tale of Despair and Survival

The Micro-Mastery Method: Transform Your Skills in Just Minutes a Day

Reclaiming Time: How to Live More by Doing Less
Chronovore: The Eternal Nexus
The Mind Reset: Unlocking Your Inner Peace in a Chaotic World
Confidence Code: Building Unshakable Self-Belief
Baby the Vampire Terrier
Baby the Vampire Terrier's Christmas Adventure
Celestial Streams: The Content Creator's Astrology Manual
The Wealth Whisperer: Unlocking Abundance with Everyday Actions
The Energy Equation: Maximize Your Output Without Burning Out
The Happiness Algorithm: Science-Backed Steps to Joyful Living
Stress-Free Success: Achieving Goals Without Anxiety
Mindful Wealth: The New Blueprint for Financial Freedom
The Festive Flavors of New Year: A Culinary Celebration
The Master's Gambit: Keys of Eternal Power
Shadowed Secrets: Groundhog Day Mysteries
Beneath the Burrow: Lessons from the Groundhog
Spring's Whispers: The Groundhog's Prediction
The Limitless Mindset: Unlock Your Untapped Potential
The Focus Funnel: How to Cut Through Chaos and Get Results
Bold Moves: Building Courage to Live on Your Terms
The Daily Shift: Simple Practices for Lasting Transformation
The Quarter-Life Reset: Thriving in Your 20s and 30s
The Art of Shadowplay: Building Your Own Personal Myth
The Eternal Loop: Finding Purpose in Repetition
Burrowing Wisdom: Life Lessons from the Groundhog
Shadow Work: A Groundhog Day Perspective
Love in Bloom: 5-Minute Romantic Gestures
The Shadowspell Codex: Secrets of Forbidden Magick
The Burnout Cure: Finding Balance in a Busy World
The Groundhog Prophecy: Unlocking Seasonal Secrets
Nog Tales: The Spirited History of Eggnog

Six More Weeks: Embracing Seasonal Transitions
The Lumivian Chronicles: Fragments of the Fifth Dimension
Money on Your Mind: A Beginner's Guide to Wealth
The Focus Fix: Breaking Through Distraction
January's Spirit Keepers: Mystical Protectors of the Cold
Creativity Unchained: Unlocking Your Wildest Ideas in 2025
Manifestation Mastery: 365 Days to Rewrite Your Reality
The Groundhog's Mirror: Reflecting on Change
The Weeping Angels' Christmas Curse
Burrowed in Time: A Groundhog Day Journey
Heartbeats: Poems to Share with Your Valentine
Dino Wicca: The Sacred Grimoire of Prehistoric Magick
Courage of the Pride: Finding Your Inner Roar
The Lion's Leap: Bold Moves for Big Results
Healthy Hustle: Achieving Without Overworking
Practical Manifesting: Turning Dreams into Reality in 2025
Jurassic Pharaohs: Unlocking the Magick of Ancient Egypt and Dino Wicca
The Happiness Equation: Small Changes for Big Joy
The Confidence Compass: Finding Your Inner Strength
Whispers in the Hollow: Tales of the Forgotten Beasts
Echoes from the Hollow: The Return of Forgotten Beasts
The Hollow Ascendant: The Rise of the Forgotten Beasts
The Relationship Reset: Building Better Connections
Mastering the Morning: How to Win the Day Before 8 AM
The Shadow's Dance: Groundhog Day Symbolism
Cupid's Kitchen: Quick Valentine's Day Recipes
Valentine's Day on a Budget: Love Without Breaking the Bank
Astrocraft: Aligning the Stars in the World of Minecraft
Forecasting Life: Groundhog Day Reflections
Bleeding Hearts: Twisted Tales of Valentine's Terror
Herbal Smoke Revolution: The Ultimate Guide to Nature's Cigarette Alternative

Winter's Wrath: The Complete Survival Blueprint for Extreme Freezes.

The Groundhog's Shadow: A Tale of Seasons

Burrowed Insights: Wisdom from the Groundhog

Sensual Strings: The Art of Erotic Bondage

Whispered Flames: Unlocking the Power of Fire Play

Forgotten Shadows: A Guide to Cryptids Lost to Time

Six Weeks of Secrets: Groundhog Day's Hidden Messages

Shadows and Cycles: Groundhog Day Reflections

The Art of Love Letters: Crafting the Perfect Message

Romantic Getaways at Home: Turning Your Space into Paradise

Purrfect Brews: A Cat Lover's Guide to Coffee and Companionship

The Groundhog's Wisdom: Timeless Lessons for Modern Life

The Shadow Oracle: Groundhog Day as a Predictor

Emerging from the Burrow: A Journey of Renewal

The Language of Love: Learning Your Partner's Love Style

Authorpreneur: The Ultimate Blueprint for Writing, Publishing, and Thriving as an Author

Weathering the Seasons: Groundhog Day Perspectives

Valentine's Day Magic: A Guide to Romantic Rituals

The Shadow Chronicles: Stories of Groundhog Day

Love and Laughter: Fun Games for Valentine's Day

AstroRealty: Unlocking the Stars for Property Success

The Groundhog's Path: A Guide to Seasonal Balance

Groundhog Day Diaries: Reflections in the Shadow

The Groundhog's Light: Illuminating the Path Ahead

Valentine's Traditions from Around the World

AI Wealth Revolution: Unlocking the Trillionaire Mindset

Love Rekindled: Reigniting Passion in Relationships

Single and Thriving: Self-Love on Valentine's Day

Emerald Legends: Mystical Tales of Ireland

Green Alchemy: Harnessing Nature's Magic
The Hearts of Horror: A Valentine's Day Nightmare
The Leprechaun's Guide to Wealth and Wisdom
Dancing with the Sidhe: Celebrating the Otherworld
Shamrocks and Shadows: Mysteries of the Green Isle
Emerald Energy: Harnessing Luck and Growth
The Gingerbread Golem's Valentine: A Sweetheart's Guide to Love and Enchantment
The Celtic Knot: Weaving Life and Destiny
Green Fire: Elemental Magic for St. Patrick's Day
Clover Chronicles: Finding Your Inner Luck
Ireland's Mystical Creatures: A Field Guide
Gingerbread Golem's Love Almanac
Prowl and Thrive: The Lion's Guide to Success
Love Alchemy: Transforming Your Life Through Heart Energy
WORLD DOMINATION: Woman's Rule 3:The New Life
The Midnight Rose: A Guide to Lunar Love Spells
The Forbidden Letters: Writing Your Own Love Prophecy
Luck and Lore: St. Patrick's Day for Modern Mystics
The Green Path: A Pagan Celebration of Renewal
The Dark Architect's Guide to Reprogramming Reality
Prankster's Paradise: A Guide to Harmless Hijinks
Manifest Your Reality: The Law of Attraction Simplified
The TARDIS Owner's Manual: Understanding the Doctor's Ship: *A complete guide to the TARDIS, its technology, secrets, and mysteries*
Starlit Romance: Astrology Secrets for Finding True Love
The Time Lord's Atlas: A Complete Guide to the Whoniverse: ***A breakdown of the locations, planets, and dimensions explored in Doctor Who***
Sweetheart Shadows: The Dark Side of Love and Attraction
February Fire: Reigniting Passion in Every Area of Life

The Self-Love Toolkit: 5 Ways to Embrace Who You Are
February Sparks: Ignite Your Dreams in 28 Days
March to Success: A 31-Day Action Blueprint
Ancient Paths: The 13 Sacred Principles of Dino Wicca
Echoes of Tomorrow: Navigating the AI Revolution
The Wellness Blueprint: Balancing Mind, Body, and Soul
Green Horizons: Sustainable Living for a Better Tomorrow
The AI Wealth Code: How to Make Millions with Automation
AI-Powered Creativity: Writing, Art, and Music for Profit
Extinction Rites: Rebirthing Your Soul Through Prehistoric Magick
Sacred Serpents tarot
Celestial Enchantment blank journal
Star Strains
Culinary Journeys: Exploring Global Flavors at Home
The Hollowvale Curse
The Hollowvale Harvest
The Egg of Transformation: Awakening Your Inner Power
Blooming Into Power: A Wiccan Guide to Spring Awakening
The Nightmare Nexus: The Third Doctor's Perilous Haunting
Digital Detox: Reclaiming Your Life in a Connected World
Ostara's Path: Walking the Spiral of Renewal
The Sacred Hare
Financial Freedom: Building Wealth in the Modern Age
Spring's Cauldron: Stirring the Waters of Change
The Hollowvale Pact
Quantum Consciousness: The Science of Reality Shifting
The Hollowvale Hunger
The Sacred Waters Within: A Witch's Guide to Hydrocephalus Magick
The Raven's Nest: Building a Life of Unshakable Stability
AI and the Human Mind: The Future of Intelligence
The Hollowvale Reckoning

Timeless Love: Building and Maintaining Lasting Relationships

The Raven's Roar: Unlocking Unstoppable Confidence

Raven Sight: Awakening Intuition and Inner Wisdom

The Butterfly Effect: Small Changes, Big Transformations

Taming the Boogeyman: How to Conquer Your Inner Fears

The Magick of Green: Awakening Earth's Energy in You

The Entrepreneurial Mindset: Secrets to Business Success

The Hollowvale End

The Shadow Luck Ritual: Reclaiming Power from Your Dark Side

Spring Magick for Beginners: A Simple Guide to Seasonal Energy Work

Doctor Who: The Hollowvale Conundrum

The March of Miracles: Unlocking Synchronicities in Spring

Unveiling the Cosmos: A Guide to Stargazing and Space Exploration

The Ultimate Guide to Surviving an Economic Collapse

The AI Gold Rush: How to Profit from the AI Revolution

Bastet's Shadow: The Hidden Power of Feline Magick

The Bastet Codex: Unlocking the Goddess's Magickal Secrets

Purring Spells: Harnessing Bastet's Healing Frequencies

Bastet's Nine Lives: Rebirth, Transformation, and Immortality Spells

Primal Currents: Hydrocephalus Magick in the Path of Dino Wicca

The Digital Gold Rush: Mastering E-Commerce and Online Sales

Future Shock: Adapting to the Next Decade of Change

The Quantum Mindset: Think Like a Billionaire

Sacred Motherhood: Awakening the Divine Feminine Within

The Mother's Spellbook: Enchantments for Love, Protection, and Prosperity

The Witch's Guide to Parenting: Raising Empowered and Intuitive Children

The Magick of Motherhood: Reclaiming Your Power Through Rituals

The Pagan Path to Self-Love: A Goddess's Guide to Worth and Confidence

Wild Woman Magick: Unleashing Your Primal Power

The Money Magnet Blueprint: Unlocking Unlimited Wealth

Biohacking 101: Unlock Your Body's Full Potential

The Wild Father: A Pagan Guide to Strength and Wisdom

The Sacred Masculine: Unlocking Your Inner Power

The Druid's Compass

The Warrior's Mindset

The Father's Fire

Odin's Path

Ancestral Bonds

The House That Whispers

The Magician's Code

The Wild Hunt

The Green Man's Path

The Altar of Success

The Shadow and the Sword

The High Priestess's Guide to Energy Healing

The Lunar Mother

The Sacred Self-Care Grimoire

The Womb Wisdom Codex

The Wheel of the Mother

The Witch's Guide to Manifestation

The Q2 Reset

The Ultimate Guide to AI-Powered Passive Income

Escape the 9-5

AI Feline Fortunes

The Tear-Stained Grimoire

Razorblade Runes
Cemetery Sirens
The Midnight Wristwatch
The Town That Forgets
AI Horror & Creepypasta
The Hollow Frequency
The Breach Echo
The Quiet Between Worlds
The Sigil of Tharan-Khul
Summon the Vault of Y'ha'ten
The Becoming Codex
The Profit of Az'ra-nar
The Drowned Logos
Echoes of the Eldritch Will
The Deep Ledger
Necronomicon of Networth
Covenant of the Wealthwyrm
The Whisperer's Manifesto
The Rites of Azh-K'luth
The Ark of the Crawling Coin
The Tithe of Shadows
Inkheart Abyss
The Timewinds of Y'ha-nthlei
The Spiral Labyrinth of Azag-Nirrh
The Gallifreyan Heresy of the Black Pharaoh
The Psalms of Nyog-Sotha
Black Rain Alchemy
The Infinite Maw
The Entropic Blueprint
The Oracle of Sh'guul
The Book of Breach
The Drowned Saint's Testament
Dreamcraft of the Sleeper God

The Silence Market
Cthonomics: The Dark Wealth Algorithm
Invocation of the Ten-Eyed King
Wealthbound to the Wyrm Below
Become the Unnameable
Codex of the Sovereign Flame
Rituals of Relentless Becoming
The Shadow Ascends
The Eyes Beneath You
The Will That Wakes Worlds
Silence Is a Weapon
The Mirror That Screams
The Whisper Between Moments
The Mind That Devours Fear
The Myth of the Finished Self
The Architect of Your Madness
The Voice You've Buried
The Discipline of Madness
Stormborn: Awakening Your Inner Tempest
The Mind That Ate Time
Unbind Your Becoming
The Pact You Owe Yourself
The Devourer's Diet
The Acid That Carves the Path
The Tower You Must Burn
The Breath Between Worlds
Speak Like the Deep
The Labyrinth Within
The Spine of the Sea God
Rejection Is a Portal
The Crown You Refused
The Scar Is the Spell
The Lightless Flame

The Habit of Becoming Horrific
ChickenJockey Chaos
The Gatekeeper Within
You Are Not Your Name
The Compass of the Mad
The Archive of Unsent Letters
What the Mirror Can't Show You
The Knife You Needed
Worship Nothing, Become Everything
The Other Voice
The Body the World Forgot
The Vein of the Void
The Black Bone Codex
The Puzzle of the Hidden Self (Millennium Puzzle)
The Eye That Sees the Lie *(Millennium Eye)*
The Ring of Return (Millennium Ring)
The Rod of Relentless Will ***(Millennium Rod)***
The Tally of the Soul (Millennium Tauk/Necklace)
The Key to the Locked Timeline (Millennium Key)
The Scale of Sacred Decisions (Millennium Scales)
Inferno Bites: The UnOfficial Minecraft Lava Cookbook
Rot in the Attic
Prana: The Hidden Force of Your Infinite Self
The Shadow Realm Within: Transforming Darkness Into Destiny
The Borderland Collapse
Claws of Protection: Bastet's Defensive Magick
Mr. Ring-a-Ding's Madness
Yugioh Astrology: Celestial Deckcraft and Duel Destiny (2026–2027 Edition)
The Seal You Signed: Unlocking the Power You Once Feared
The Puzzle of Infinite Minds: Unlocking the Mentalism Hidden Within

The Eye That Mirrors the All: Secrets of Inner Reflection
Doctor Who: The Toymaker's Broadcast
The Rod of Eternal Flow: Commanding the Currents of Vibration
Golden Eyes of Bastet: Enhancing Psychic Vision
The Key of Dual Forces: Balance Within the Polarity
The Scales of Living Rhythm: Timing the Dance of Life
The Necklace of Hidden Cause: Weaving the Webs of Fate
The Ring of Secret Masters: Rising Through the All Within All
Daggers of the Dying Deep
Bastet's Wealth and Fortune Magick: Prosperity Rituals of the Goddess
The Tide that Speaks
The Scrolls of Petosiris: 13 Rituals from the Feathered Eye
Petosiris and the Living Plague of Osirion
Feline Fire: Bastet's Passion and Love Magick
The Star Altar of Petosiris
Bastet's Whiskers: Supernatural Sensory Magick
The Bastet Grimoire
Feeding the Shadows
The Mouthless Prayer
The Spiral Wound
Becoming the Ibis: Lessons from Petosiris's Mind
The Crimson Coven: Cola Magick for Sweet Dominion
Sacred Cat's Paw
The Soda Zodiac: A Flavor for Every Sign
Covenant of the Crawling Flame
The Ink of Ish'Zur
Frothroot: The Thirst That Ate the World
The Golden Glyphs of Prosperity
The Etherbind Codex
Echoes of the Resistance: Reclaiming the You That Survived

Harnessed Minds: Breaking Free from Mental Control
The Eyes in the Smoke
Rootwake: The Carbon Covenant
Skitter Logic: Unlearning the Fear That Built You
Doctor Who: The World That Froths
Rootwake: The Fizz That Rewrites Flesh
Rootwake: Frothfather of the World
The Holly Pact: Blood Beneath the Mistletoe
The 2nd Mass Principle: Building Unbreakable Tribes
Web of Wits: A Survival Guide to Encounters with Anasi the Spider (Aunt Nancy)
The Hexbreaking Handbook: Effective Spells to Remove Curses
Pop Alchemy: Transform Your Life One Sip at a Time
The Mason Code: Leading in Unleadable Times
Petosiris and the Fifth Chamber of Thoth
The Ether Seed Within
The Parent of Tomorrow
Petosiris's Pyramid of Perpetual Wealth
Unlearn the World
Grimoire of the Hollow Tongue
Zodiac Weeds: Finding Your Strain Through the Stars
Aquarius Rises in the Bank
The Sugar God's Smile
The Skinclock Reversal: Biohacking the Face of Time
Debtburn: How to Obliterate What You Owe Forever
The Ice Cream Oracle: What Your Cone Says About Your Future
Silence Is Sovereignty: The Power of Being Unreadable
The Wind That Whispers Through Stone
Path of the Four Directions
Doctor Who: The Maestro's Symphony of Endings
Oxygen Grail: Breathing to Undo the Clock

Zodiacal Collapse: When Stars Devour Time
Teachings from the Red Sand Silence
Doctor Who: Omega – The Broken Equation
Memory Wipe Your Past: Start Over Like a MiB
Mitochondria Prime: Ignite the Core of Youth
A Nest of Roaches
Grub from the Galaxy: MiB Recipes You'll Never Forget
Whiskers of Power: Bastet's Guide to Inner Sovereignty
The Gift Must Cost Them: Negotiation Through Unequal Exchange
The Worm Guys' Wealth Code: Hustle Like an Alien
Bug Out: The Edgar Method for Ruthless Goal Setting
Weaving Life with Spiderwoman's Pattern
Doctor Who: The Rani's Renaissance
How to Get a Job (If You're a Puppygirl)
Speak Through Others: The Art of Proxy Power
T-Rex Your Trauma: Reclaim the Power of Your Primal Self
The Black Briefcase: How MiB Stay Wealthy in Silence
The Thirst Beyond Reason: Understanding Diabetes Insipidus From the Inside Out
Backwoods Witchcraft for Billionaires: The Pagan Path from Dirt Roads to Gold Roads
The Moonshine Grimoire: Fermented Spells for Abundance
The Nameless Geometry
The Wraith's Mixtape: Spellcasting with Songs of Sorrow
The Gallifreyan Gentleman: Silent Wealth, Sonic Confidence, and the Doctor's Code of Living
Sugar Water Confidence
Dino Totems: Spirit Guides from Earth's First Gods
Pumpkin Sigils & Ritual Smoke
The Hózhó Compass
The Distortus Discipline – Order from Inner Mutation
Witchcraft for the Cold-Blooded Soul

Moonlight Over the Blessingway
Water, Interrupted: When the Body Forgets How to Hold On
Deformed but Divine: Embracing Your Asymmetry
Hexes in the Henhouse: The Farm Witch's Guide to Power
The Reversed Flame: A Grimoire of Inverted Power
Salt, Cells, and Sanity: Reclaiming Balance with Diabetes Insipidus
King of the Broken: Crowning the Flawed Self
Moonlight Scars: Emo Moon Magick and the Art of Lunar Sorrow
Noose Spells: Magick of the Hanging Rope
The Goth Cathedral: Rituals of the Broken and Beautiful
The Cretaceous Codex: Dino Spirits and Fossil Magick
The Turkey Bones Ritual
Nine Lives of Manifestation: Unlocking Bastet's Reality Codes
Chaos Muscles: Building Strength from Twisted Pain
Emo Blood Magick: The Veins of Power
The 3AM Flood: Nighttime Urination, Sleep Loss, and the DI Spiral
The Silence Between the Stars
The Lemon Method: Sour Your Way to Success
Starlit Sovereign
The Rite of Twelve Gates: Walking the Gates of the Duat.
Cornbread and Conjure: Recipes for Riches and Rootwork
The Black Rose Rituals: Emo Love Spells and Obsession Magick
The Eternal Goodbye: Death Magick and Rebirth Rituals
Sinkrot: The Drain That Remembers
The Hybrid Mindset: Thinking Beyond Evolution
Bone Dry: Navigating Dehydration Before It Breaks You
Wreathcraft: Winter Sigils and Yuletide Spells
The Rite of Twelve Mouths

S'mores of the Damned: Haunted Recipes for Halloween Night

Rethink the Drink: A Beverage Survival Guide for DI Warriors

The Shadow Chord: Guitar Magick and Sonic

Malformed Yet Majestic: Leading When You Feel Wrong Inside

The Cursed Diary: Ink-Stained Spells of the Emo Soul

Anxiety Off Switch: Emergency Reset for a Fried Nervous System

The Energy Heist: How to Take Back Your Life from Drainers

Beyond the Bathroom: Rebuilding Your Social Life With DI

Coyote's Gift for Decision Makers

Ghoul-Goo: Spooky S'mores You'll Die For

Echoes in the Mirror: Scrying and Self-Destruction Magick

Thread and Thorn: Stitching Spells from Rural Cloth

The Mogwai Mind: Building Untouchable Wealth from Small Ideas

Be Your Own Guide: Trust Your Inner Compass

Hormones in Chaos: The Endocrine Puzzle of Diabetes Insipidus

ChronoCleanse: Detox Your Biological Timeline

The Limb You Hide Is the One That Saves You

Leaves, Bones, and Whisper Spells

The Dinosaur Mindset: Prehistoric Tactics for Modern Wealth

Clawing Back Control: A Bastet Method for Boundaries and Empowerment

Samhain Codes of the Forgotten

Orange Alchemy: The Autumnal Spellbook

Monster Within, Master Without

The Sigil That Sleeps

Hearthcraft: Yule Hearth Sigils and Winter Warmth Spells

Temple of the Purring Moon: Rituals from Bastet's Lineage
When the Earth Remembers Your Footsteps
Food for Mood: Eat to Heal Depression, Not Just Survive It
Witch of the Kudzu Vine: Southern Pagan Wealth Secrets
The Invisible Diagnosis: Advocating for Yourself With DI
The Coffin's Lullaby: Sleep Magick and Nightmares as Portals
Ashes of the Will: Rituals for Erasing the Self
The Fracture Rite: Shattering the Magickal Core
Funeral Candles: The Art of Emo Flame Magick
The Black Grimoire: A Blank Ritual for Writing in Absence
Phantom Thirst: A Halloween Survival Guide for Diabetes Insipidus
The Hollow Crown: Emo Royalty and Magick of the Outcast King
Sandpainting for the Soul
Falling Into Balance: Using the Extra Hour to Recalibrate Life
100 Southern Superstitions That Still Work
The DI Child: A Parent's Guide to Raising Hydrated, Happy Kids
The Jungle of Shame: Escaping the Hidden Lab of Doubt
The Witch's Toast: S'mores Spells and Creepy Confections
The Hoodoo Pantry: Spells from the Mason Jar
The Immortal Fortune: Secret Wealth Lessons from Captain Jack Harkness
The Specter's Embrace: Magick for Channeling Ghostly Lovers
Grateful Waters: A Thanksgiving Survival Guide for Diabetes Insipidus
The Seizure Gospel
Harvestbind: Autumn Sigils and Samhain Spells
Doctor Who: The Algorithmic Awakening
Silent Nights, Steady Waters: A Christmas Survival Guide for Diabetes Insipidus

The Extra Hour Effect: How One Hour Can Transform Everything

Blade Between the Breaths

Running with the Mountain Shadows

Echoes of the Failed Experiment – Becoming a Living Legacy

Swamp Witches & River Ghosts: Real Southern Hauntings

Cornbread Prophecies: Magical Recipes from a Southern Table

Doctor Who: The Signal in the Star

Bloomcraft: Spring Sigils and Equinox Enchantments

Vanisher: How to Disappear from the Internet Without Losing Your Life

The Ultimate Christmas Cookie Cookbook

The Unbreakable Parent: How to Mentally Survive Raising Kids in a Broken World

Time Debt: How to Reclaim the Hours You Didn't Know You Lost

One Month, One Million: Unconventional Cash Creation Tactics

Doctor Who: The Cyber Conversion Protocol

Black Friday Frenzy: The Art of Finding Hidden Online Deals

The Grimoire Buried Under the Apple Tree

Digital Couponing Masterclass: Your Step-by-Step Guide to Black Friday Savings

The Fire Inside the Flint

Shadows on the Ceiling: The Emo Guide to Astral Magick

The Bone-Eaters Beneath Us

Black Friday Bundle Blueprint: Creating Irresistible Product Packages for Maximum Sales

Thirteen Nights of Unbinding

Doctor Who: Engines of Influence

Pumpkin Spice Alchemy: Recipes of Fire and Frost

When Raptor Met Rexy: Prehistoric Lessons in Wild Romance
Oblivion's Candle: Burn the Path Behind You
Campfire Curses and Chocolate: A Halloween S'mores Grimoire
The Wallet That Wasn't Mine: Breaking Free from Inherited Scarcity
The Cola Zodiac: What Your Fizz Says About Your Fate
Frostfire Fortune: Unlocking Winter's Hidden Prosperity
Signal Jamming: Detox Your Brain from Info Overload
The Dust of the Forgotten Rite
The Golden Cat Sigils: Drawing Power in Bastet's Name
Mud Magick: The Prosperity of Getting Dirty
Savory Spicefall: Beyond the Pumpkin Pie
Pumpkin Spice Apothecary Kitchen
The Pumpkin Spice Economy: Turning Trends into Billions
The Ember Veil: 13 Nights of Fire Magick
Financial Freeze: When Earning Triggers Panic
The Gingerbread Alchemist: Sweet Recipes with a Twist
Biosynth Power: Programming Yourself from Scratch
Echoes from the Talking Circle
Truffle Alchemy: Fungus of Fortune
Spores of Power: The Truffle Witch's Handbook
Doctor Who: The Tower That Speaks
The Mycelium Veil: Truffle Magick Unbound
Broke But Ashamed: Healing the Shame Wound of Debt
The Evergreen Mind: Growth Through Winter Stillness
The Black Veil Truffle Rite
The Voice Beneath Symbols
Witchlight on the Bayou: Swamp Spells for Sovereignty
I Grew Up Poor and Now I Sabotage My Success
The Lantern of Hollow Souls

Shutdown Survival: A Citizen's Guide to Thriving When Government Stops

When Abundance Feels Like a Threat: Healing the Hidden Fears of Enough

The Scarecrow Grimoire

Owls of the October Veil

Candlewax and Curses: A Halloween Spellbook

Excavating the Inner Fossil – Transforming Fossilized Thoughtforms into Tools of Power

The Yule Witch's Spellbook: Magick for the Holiday Season

Haunted Christmas: Ghost Stories for Winter Nights

The Christmas Survival Guide: Thriving Through the Chaos

The Bone Orchard Rites

Haunted Commerce: The Ghost in the Marketplace

When Money Triggers the Inner Child

Silent Night with the Silence: A Christmas Thriller

The Lightning Crown: Living and Leading Through Seizures

TARDIS Tidings: Festive Stories from the Whoniverse

Autumn Reset: Slowing Down Without Falling Behind

The Trillion Dollar Soul: Rewriting the Currency of Reality

Truffle Eclipse Magick

Micro-Manifestations: Quick Magick That Works

5-Minute Rituals for Busy Witches

The Marshmallow Massacre: Halloween Treats with a Sinister Twist

Blood and Blackberry Thorns

Magickal Mornings: Rituals for a Blessed Christmas Day

Embers of the All-Hallows Fire

The Pumpkin Market Collapse

The Hour You Gained: Transforming Time Into Power

The Chamber Must Be Sealed: Mastering the Power of Controlled Access

The Cursed Manuscript of Petosiris

The Festive Hearth: Creating Holiday Traditions
Darkness Rising: Thriving as Nights Grow Longer
Harvesting Time: Turning the Year's End Into Your New Beginning
Petosiris and the 13th Zodiac Key
Wagewound: When Paychecks Become Identity Prisons
Walls That Watch
The Silent Feast: Rituals of Power in the Longest Night
The Distortus Legacy : Becoming a Deformed King in a Perfect World
The Hollow Masks
The Gratitude Furnace: Forging Gold from Thanks
Feast of Inner Gold: Eating for Energy and Enlightenment
Haunted Commerce: The Season of Spending Spirits
Fear Bonds: How Panic Creates Profit
Black Friday E-Commerce Playbook: Sales Tactics to Skyrocket Your Holiday Revenue
Budgeting for Black Friday: A Holiday Savings Planner
Haunting the Harvest Moon
The Warrior's Water: Emergency Preparedness for People With DI
The First Sip of the Year: A New Year's Survival Guide for Diabetes Insipidus
Doctor Who: The Thirteenth Node
The Unseen Struggle: Mental Health, Anxiety, and Chronic Thirst
The Hearth's Hidden Ledger: Counting Energies as Currency
The Gift Alchemist: Turning Any Offering Into Gold
The Papyrus of the Bound Spirit
The Magick of Leftovers: Transmutation in the Fridge
Frost and Fortune: Christmas Wealthcraft for the Modern Magus
Last-Minute Gifts: Creative Ideas on a Budget

10 Secrets to Surviving Holiday Crowds
The Witch's Dow Jones
The Witches' Graveyard Shift
Pumpkin Sigils: Carving Rites for Midnight Power
The Secret Shopper's Black Friday Guide: How to Get Early Access and VIP Deals
Fever in the Foundation
The Neuralyzer Reset: Reprogram Your Morning Routine
Lightning Lessons of the White Painted Woman
The Enchanted Snowflake
The Magic Sip: Surviving Disney Parks with Diabetes Insipidus
The One Who Draws Through You
Santa's Secrets: A Magical Holiday Planner
Silent Bells, Loud Miracles: Self-Help for the Season of Stillness
The Sugar Spell Codex: Confectionary Magick of Christmas
Autumn Hexcraft: Fallen Leaves, Fallen Barriers
Sleep Like a Fortress: Build a Life Where Insomnia Can't Survive
Nowhere Was Ever Home
Christmas Under the Stars: A Celestial Holiday Guide
Rentproof: How to Never Be Evicted Again
Workless: Escape the 9-5 Without Being Broke
The Gilded Gift: A Wealth Altar for Christmas Morning
The Black Friday Grimoire
The Hollowing: Ceremonies of Spiritual Collapse
Doctor Who: The Nameless Signal
Where the Eagle Hides His Courage
The Dwarf Tyrant's Ascent: Claiming Power in a World of Giants
The Currency of the Dead: Trading with Spectral Bankers
The Icebound Witch: Survival and Magick in the Cold

The Emergency Money Mind: Constant Crisis, Zero Calm

Thirst & Roses: A Valentine's Survival Guide for Diabetes Insipidus

Springing Into Clarity: Mastering the Energy Shift of Daylight Saving

Speed of the Nanotyrant: Agile Strategies for Life's Hunt

The 90-Day Reset: A Science-Backed Guide to Reinvent Yourself Before the New Year

The Coil of Thorns

Timegates Unleashed

Dopamine Fasting 2.0: Rewiring Your Brain in a World of Overstimulation

The Nanotyrannus Mutation: Embracing Your Differentiated Form

Unwritten January: How to Use the Blank Page of the Year to Re-Author Your Life

Feast of the Forgotten Spirits: Ancestor Magick for the Holidays

The Burnout Codex: A System for Thriving Beyond Stress

I Don't Deserve to Have Money

When the King Doesn't See You: The Shadow Predator's Guide

The Reset Ritual :A Guide to Shedding Last Year's Weight—Emotional and Physical—by Spring Cleaning Your Soul

Calendar Alchemy: Learn to Bend Time and Productivity around Your Natural Rhythms

The Mirror Contract: A One-Sentence Agreement with Yourself that Unlocks Real Change

The Nile Formula: Sacred Flow for Millionaire Minds

Forward Momentum: Productivity Rituals for the Lost Hour

Harvest Gold: Wealth Magick of Pumpkin Spice Commerce

The Magick of Christmas Lights: Illuminating Holiday Rituals

Cranberry Crown: Royal Self-Worth through Ritual Meals

Petosiris and the Worms of the Feathered Throne

The Evergreen Equation: Self-Help for Sustained Growth

The Rain Will Wash Us Away: Emo Weather Magick

Snowlight Shadows: Magick Under Frozen Stars

Doctor Who: Merger of Empires

The Light Within the Feast: Magickal Wealth of Yuletide Flame

Momentum Machines: Small Habits Designed to Snowball into Unstoppable Forward Motion

Calm Spells: Magickal Solutions for Anxiety Relief

Santa's Final List: The Naughty Never Leave

The Mystic's Guide to Banishing Worry

The Silence Dividend: Turning Quiet Mornings into Compounding Growth All Year

Charmed Stillness: Rituals to Ease the Mind

Blood Spiral Ascension

The Vanishing Heart Invocation

Crystal Calm: Harnessing Stones for Anxiety

The Nano Tyrant Code: Strength in the Small Predator

The Energy Ledger: Accounting Methods for Vitality, Not Just Money

Snowglobe Mindset: Shake Up Your Thoughts, Settle Into Peace

The Weight of the Feather: Anubis's Codes for Soul Balance

Pocket Peppermint Power: Tiny Rituals for Big Holiday Energy

Shadowkeeper of the Golden Jackal: Anubis's Path to Energetic Protection

The Witch's Breath: Anxiety Relief Through Magickal Breathing

The Tiny Ember: Pocket Motivation for Cold Days

Stocking Sorcery: Mini Spells for Holiday Luck and Prosperity

Warm Hands, Steady Heart: Micro Grounding for Winter Anxiety

The Jackal's Lantern: Guide-Lights for Walking the Dark Path

Anubis's Silent Steps: Rituals for Stealth, Peace & Emotional Quiet

The Bonewake Protocol

Extinction-Proof: How to Outlive Trends, Trauma, and Time

The Fourth Doctor: The Eccentric Wanderer

The Second Doctor: Chaos and Charm in the TARDIS (Patrick Troughton, 1966–1969)

The Third Doctor: Earthbound Defender of Time (Jon Pertwee, 1970–1974)

The First Doctor: Genesis of the Time Lord (William Hartnell, 1963–1966)

The Fourth Doctor: The Eccentric Wanderer ***(Tom Baker, 1974–1981)***

The Fifth Doctor: Elegance and Empathy (Peter Davison, 1982–1984)

The Sixth Doctor: A Kaleidoscope of Conflict (Colin Baker, 1984–1986)

The Seventh Doctor: The Strategist of Shadows (Sylvester McCoy, 1987–1989)

The Eighth Doctor: A Time Lord's Renaissance (Paul McGann, 1996)

The War Doctor: A Time Lord's Burden (John Hurt, 2013)

The Ninth Doctor: The Healer of Worlds
(Christopher Eccleston, 2005)

The Tenth Doctor: The Lonely Hero (David Tennant, 2005–2010)

The Eleventh Doctor: The Madman in a Box (Matt Smith, 2010–2013)

The Twelfth Doctor: The Rebel with a Cause (Peter Capaldi, 2013–2017)

The Thirteenth Doctor: Breaking the Mold
(Jodie Whittaker, 2017–2022)

The Fourteenth Doctor: A New Beginning (David Tennant, 2022–2023)

The Fifteenth Doctor: Rewriting the Stars
(Ncuti Gatwa, 2023–2025)

Santa's Shortcut to Success: Micro Habits for a Better New Year

The Midnight Cocoa Manifesto: Comfort Rituals for Hard Nights

Why I Can't Save: Trauma Blocks to Financial Planning

Dino Brain, Mega Goals: Rewire Yourself for Savage Success.

Jurassic Profit: Unearth Your Inner Millionaire Fossil

Scales & Softness: Dating with Dino Heart

Carnotaurus Dreams.

Red Willow Thinking.

Reindeer Resilience: How to Keep Going When You're Exhausted

Candlewick Courage: Lighting Strength in Dark Seasons.

Elf-Mode Focus: Fast Attention Fixes for Busy Seasons

Futureproof Feelings: Emotional Skill-Building for Resilience No Matter What the New Year Brings

The 90-Day Rewire: Transform Your Neural Pathways Before Spring Blooms

Jolly Rich: Christmas Micro-Money Magick for Fast Prosperity.

Gingerbread Gratitude: Mini Practices for a Happier Holiday

Trauma-Spending: When Money Becomes a Drug

Goal Skeletons: Build Minimalist Frameworks for Resolutions That Last

The Snarl Strategy: Growling Back at a World That Silenced You

The Hourglass Reset: Reclaiming What the Clock Took

Yule Claw: Dino Rites of Light in the Darkness

Sacred Circles: Grounding Rituals for Anxious Souls

Clockstopper's Gut: Rebuilding the Core of Time

Winterfire Drive: Harness the Cold Season's Stillness to Ignite Deep Motivation

The 5-Minute Productivity Hack: Small Steps to Big Results

Light Ascending: A Self-Help Guide to Longer Days

Inner Economy: Trade Self-Doubt for Confidence Like a High-Value Currency

Simple Success: Decluttering Your Life for Better Results

The Resilient Mind: Thriving in Tough Times

The 2026 Playbook: Mastering the Year Ahead

The Spring Sleep Solution: Conquering Fatigue After Time Change.

The Hormonal Compass: Navigate Back to Your Youth

Golden Vision: Eating for Your Eye Color with the Power of Ghee

Lionhearted Love: Strength in Relationships

MiB Mindset: Think Like a Cosmic Agent

The Ladder of Small Wins: Climb Out of Stagnation by Stacking Micro-Victories

The Momentum Hour: Gaining More in Less Time.

The Year of You: A Self-Help Blueprint for Unapologetic Self-Ownership

The Dust That Watches You Back.

The Astral Parent

Shadow of the King: The Nanotyrannus Parable

Tiny Tidings of Triumph: Small Wins That Change Your Life

Dwarf Tyrant Rising: When You're the One They Overlook

The Bank Account Mirror: Healing How You See Yourself Through Money
Cretaceous Black
When Love Costs Too Much: Romantic Triggers and Financial Wounds
Dream-Eater's Guide to Wealth
Unzipped Reality: The Jacket That Opens Portals
The Power of No: How to Set Boundaries and Get Rich
Keeper of the Desert Veil: Anubis's Teachings on Illusion & Truth
Redacted Stargates: Stories the SGC Buried
The Clock That Dripped Time
Doctor Who: The Silent Acquisition
Hairline Manifestation: Unlocking Power at the Edge of Thought
Cash-Eater Crickets: How Insects Predict Economic Collapse
Dead Pet Whisperer: Grief Alchemy from the Other Side
The Love Algorithm Is Broken: Hack Romance Before It Hacks You
The Rite of the 8-Limbed Seal
Melt the Moon: A Fire Ritual to Reshape Emotion
Venomous Miracles: Healing Through the Poison Path
Wealth Without Water: The Post-Aquatic Rich Life
The Butterfly Betrayal: When Change Turns on You
The Quiet Upgrade: How Humans Are Secretly Rebuilding Themselves Without Asking Permission

Get Some Tarot cards: https://www.makeplayingcards.com/sell/apophis-occult-shop

Get some shirts: https://www.bonfire.com/store/apophis-shirt-emporium/

Instagrams:
@apophis_enterprises,
@apophisbookemporium,
@apophisscardshop
Twitter: @apophisenterpr1
Tiktok:@apophisenterprise
Youtube: @sg1fan23477
Hive: @sg1fan23477
CheeLee: @SG1fan23477

Podcast: Apophis Chat Zone: https://open.spotify.com/show/5zXbrCLEV2xzCp8ybrfHsk?si=fb4d4fdbdce44dec

Newsletter: https://apophiss-newsletter-27c897.beehiiv.com/

If you want to support me or see posts of other projects that I have come over to: **buymeacoffee.com/mpetchinskg**

I post there daily several times a day

www.ingramcontent.com/pod-product-compliance
Lightning Source LLC
LaVergne TN
LVHW022008200926
848481LV00007B/2281
9798295502712